HON
Pure and Na

Daphne Metland

The Boots Company Plc Nottingham England

Published on behalf of
The Boots Company PLC,
Nottingham, England by
W. Foulsham & Company Limited
Yeovil Road, Slough, Berkshire, SL1 4JH

ISBN 0-572-01340-X

Photoset in Great Britain by
Sprint Productions Ltd.
and printed in Spain by Cayfosa, Barcelona
Dep. Leg. B. 28801/85

Reproduction of beeskep jar on front cover by kind
permission of Honey Farmers Ltd., Scotland

CONTENTS

INTRODUCTION

What is honey? – the honey bee – types of honey – set and liquid honey – honey products – honey production

The honey we all know and enjoy starts life with the honey bee. The honey bee collects nectar, a solution of water and sugars, from plants and carries it, in her honey sac, back to the hive. Within the bee's body the process of turning nectar into honey begins. Back at the hive it is stored in the cells of the comb and matured. The bees collect nectar and make honey to feed their larvae, but it can be harvested by removing the combs and draining out the honey from them.

Bees work very hard when collecting nectar. To make 500 grams of honey the bee flies the equivalent of three times around the world and uses up 75 grams of honey in flight. He will also collect enough wax from the flowers to make the intricate combs within which the honey is stored. Along the way the bees collect the pollen, which is fed to the larvae in the hives, and act as pollinators for the plants. The relationship between bees and plants is mutually beneficial; the bees get the wax and the nectar, the plants are provided with a very efficient means of cross pollination.

Once the combs are full of honey the bees cap them off with wax caps and leave them to mature. To harvest the honey the bee-keeper has to remove the combs, cut off the wax caps and drain out the honey. Traditionally this is done by leaving the frames to stand for two days, but nowadays it is more often done in a centrifuge. Once drained, the honey needs to be sieved to remove any debris and larvae. Large scale honey producers then usually subject it to a heat treatment that will allow it to be stored for long periods without crystallizing. However, care is needed not to overheat it and ruin the flavour and aroma.

THE HONEY BEE

Honey bees belong to the same group of insects as ants and wasps. In Britain the honey bee is *Apis Mellifera,* although there are other tropical honey bees with different names. Each hive is a self-contained unit, with a queen bee, drones and worker bees. Each has its own job within the hive which can consist of up to 60,000 bees.

The queen bee is, as a larvae, fed on royal jelly, a special fatty substance which is made by the worker bees. She will live for about three years and lay up to 2,000 eggs each day to provide the female worker bees and the male drones.

The drone's main purpose in life is to fertilize the queen, and each hive will have several hundred drones. The queen needs to lay unfertilized eggs to produce female worker bees and fertilized ones to produce drones.

The worker bees are the ones that go out and collect nectar and make the honey. They are also responsible for the care and up-keep of the hive, for scouting out new sources of nectar and protecting the hive from invasion.

Honey production only takes place during the summer and the bees store the honey over the winter. Production in this country is limited by our short summers but in other countries production is higher.

TYPES OF HONEY
As a natural product honey is variable. Its flavour, colour and aroma are influenced by the type of plants the bee visits. A great deal of blended honey is sold in this country but there are also about 20 different specific types of honey to choose from as well.

Blended honey
This is usually based on clover honey, but may be from varying countries in the world, depending on the harvests and the market prices. Often sold as 'own brand' honey, the manufacturer mixes the different honey to get the right flavour and colour. It is generally light and mild and good as a tea-time spread. Main producers are Australia, Canada and Chile.

Home-produced honey
This is often sold at farm shops, in local health shops or direct from the bee-keeper. The flavour will vary according to the area and crops are small so availability is variable. Worth looking out for when visiting a new area.

Comb honey

This is honey in the wooden comb. Small ones are used and then sold complete with honey and comb together. It is an expensive way to buy honey, but delicious and makes an ideal gift that is healthier for the recipient than chocolates. The comb can be eaten along with the honey or you can make a hole in it and allow the honey to trickle out.

Chunk honey

Honey in a jar, with a chunk of the comb in it. Much cheaper than buying a small comb, but with a good flavour.

Honey spreads

These can have flavouring or colouring, or glucose syrup added to them. Anything labelled 'honey' cannot, and must consist of just honey. Usually cheaper than honey and useful as a tea-time spread for children.

Flavoured honey

These can also have additives such as fruit juice, nuts, or liqueurs.

Polyflora honey

These usually specify the country of origin, but the nectar that the bees have gathered comes from a range of flowers so there is no one predominating flavour.

Organic honey

This is a bit of a misnomer, as all honey is organic in the true sense of the word, in that it is a naturally produced food. Organic is usually used to describe honeys from wild flowers. It is dark and strong-tasting.

Single source honey

Individual nectars give distinct colours and flavours to honey, so many honeys are available that include the name of the flower:

Acacia: A pale mildly flavoured unset honey that is useful in cooking. Usually from Hungary or Bulgaria.

Hymettus: Often considered the best of honeys, it is expensive as the hymettus flower grows high in the mountains. The bee-keepers have to carry the honey hives up the mountainside when the plants are in bloom and then carry them down again after the bees have collected enough nectar. It is golden-brown in colour with a strong rich taste and marvellous stirred into thick creamy natural yoghurt as the Greeks do.

Heather: This is the only honey that has a gel-like texture and often has air bubbles in it. Stir it up and it becomes liquid, but will return to the gel structure when left to stand. Dark, reddish-amber in colour with a high concentration of minerals in comparison with other honeys. Some, such as ling heather honey are bitter-sweet. Again the hives have to be moved out onto the moors when the heather is in bloom and then moved back again.

Lime blossom: Pale unset honey with a flowery taste.

Leatherwood: Light in colour but with a strong distinctive flavour.

Orange blossom: Mostly from Spain, America and South Africa, it is an amber colour with a delicate orange flavour.

Sunflower: Light and pale with a delicate flavour.

SET AND LIQUID HONEY

How runny a honey is is determined by the ratio of the two main monosaccharides in the honey, dextrose and levulose. Dextrose crystallizes out when the honey sets giving a firm set, levulose remains liquid. So honeys with a high levulose content such as Acacia and some polyflora honeys remain liquid longer.

In Britain, sales of the set and unset honey are split 50/50. Unset honey is easier to use in cooking, and the spreading honey is good for tea-time bread and scones. Some honeys are processed to make them softer to spread by heating and stirring them. Once allowed to stand they set again, but to a softer consistency.

Some honeys are encouraged to set by seeding; sprinkling with a little set honey. This is done to encourage a fine set rather than a grainy one which might naturally occur with some honeys. If honey becomes crystallized at home, it can be made liquid again by standing the jar in a pan of warm water and gently heating through. There is nothing wrong with honey like this. Some honeys become very runny if they are left on a sunny windowsill but will set again once cool.

Store honey in an airtight jar or plastic container. Do not use metal which will react with the natural acids.

7

HONEY PRODUCTS

Many products are extracted from the hive or sold as food or food supplements.

Honeycombs: These are the hexagonal cells of wax which the bees make to support the honey. Many people chew it to relieve hayfever and sinus complaints.

Honey cappings: When the honey is ripe, the bee caps the cell with a layer of wax. This has its own particular qualities, somewhat similar to honeycomb.

Propolis: This is the substance used by the bees to glue the hive together and make it weathertight. It is available in liquid and tablet form and also in pleasant-tasting sweets. Some people claim it to have antibiotic properties, and one old country remedy for sore throats suggests sucking gently on a piece of this until it dissolves.

Pollen: The pollen is collected, carefully screened of many allergic factors and made into tablets. Pollen tablets are valued by athletes in training.

Royal jelly: This is a jelly-like honey which the bees make to feed the young queen. The larvae of a worker bee can be changed into a queen if it is fed on royal jelly for the duration of its five-day larva life instead of for only three days. Royal jelly is widely used in natural cosmetics and is also marketed as a dietary supplement in liquid form and as health tablets.

Bee brood: This is made of baby bees. In some places bees do not survive the winter and the colony is killed off and the hive restocked in spring. The colony contains bee larvae and pupae, rich in vitamins A and D, and protein. The larvae are marketed as a delicacy and can be fried, smoked or grilled.

Mead: Diluted honey is fermented to make this alcoholic drink which was the traditional old English banqueting drink until the Middle Ages, when it was superseded by wine. The malic acid in mead is alleged to counteract gout and rheumatism. There are many varieties of mead, some using local berries such as the mulberry, others including wines and spices.

HONEY PRODUCTION

Home production of honey in Britain cannot meet the demand and we import a great deal of honey from Mexico, Australia, China and other countries. English honey, especially heather honeys, are in much demand abroad, so Britain also exports some honey as well.

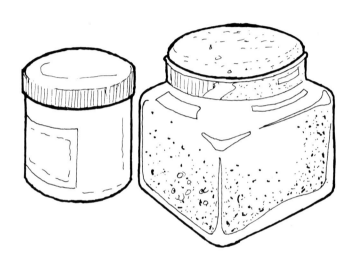

CHAPTER 1

HONEY – THE HISTORY

Honey in history and culture – collecting honey

The honey bee has been busily making honey for longer than mankind has been around to harvest it. It appears in much written history, always as a food to be sought out and used to give strength and health. Its virtues have been sung down the ages with many cultures using it to treat a whole range of ailments. Often in ancient societies the honey bee and honey were sacred. The Incas offered up honey as a sacrifice to the sun, and the ancient Egyptians used it for preserving bodies. Zeus was supposed to live on honey alone. Ambrosia, the drink of the gods, was made from honey and even now we use the word 'honeymoon' without realising that it meant literally eating honey for the first month of marriage. This was supposed to ensure a healthy life and a large family! The god of love, Eros, was believed to tip his arrows with honey to make the love all the sweeter.

Many people believe that eating honey will keep them young. There is no medical evidence for this, although from the time of the ancient Greeks until today, some people swear by the rejuvenating effects of honey.

It is often mentioned in the Bible, as in Exodus 3: 8 where the Jews are promised, 'a Land flowing with milk and honey'. In the New Testament, John the Baptist lived on honey while in the desert, 'John had his raiment of camel's hair and a leathern girdle about his loins and his meat was locusts and wild honey'. Matthew 3: 4 and Mark 1: 6.

Shakespeare accepts that you can have too much of a good thing though, 'They surfeited with honey and began to loathe the taste of sweetness, whereof a little more than a little is by much too much.' (Henry IV Part 1.)

Honey has always been considered good for invalids and children. The Roman Pliny suggested the use of honey and water as a suitable drink for invalids and a mixture of honey and vinegar, sea salt and water was used for gout and similar ailments; perhaps here the honey was needed to sweeten the medicine!

Nursery teas often consisted of bread and honey – a perfect combination if the bread is wholemeal. It appears often in children's literature and the work of adults with fond memories of tea-time treats. The most famous bear of all was addicted to honey:

'Isn't it funny how a bear likes honey?

Buzz, buzz, buzz, I wonder why he does?'

Winnie-the-Pooh obviously knew what was good for him!

Edward Lear saw fit to send the Owl and the Pussycat well equipped for all emergencies:

'They took some honey and plenty of money,

Wrapped up in a five pound note.'

Summing up the childhood love affair with honey and family tea-time is Rupert Brooke's poem full of longing for peace and home:

'Stands the clock at ten to three and is there

honey still for tea?'

Collecting Honey

Originally all bees were wild, and mankind simply collected the honey whenever he found a hive that he could reach. The bees made their colonies in holes in the ground, rock crevices and hollow trees. Many animals raid wild bees' homes, including bears and baboons, who seem to ignore the stings they receive, or who must think the honey worth the effort and pain. Primitive man hunted for honey in just the same way and Dr Eva Crane (in *A book of honey*, Oxford University Press) reports a rock painting from Spain dated around 7,000 BC showing human figures climbing up a rough ladder to reach the honey.

Gradually, though, the idea of keeping bees in hives developed. Initially it was simply a case of encouraging bees to use part of a nearby tree, perhaps by cutting a hole in the trunk. Even now bees will use almost anything that seems to be the right shape, in which to make their hives.

There have been reports of bee hives inside postboxes and even in the engine of an old car left to rust in a barn. It is highly likely that bees began to use large wicker baskets and clay pots made for other purposes. Then large containers were left out for them, either specially adapted baskets or pots, or hollowed out logs. Certainly cone-shaped wicker baskets were used widely in Medieval times and are still in use in some primitive areas today.

This type of hive can only be harvested by killing off the bees and removing the honey. Later hives were specially designed to allow the combs to be slid out and empty frames replaced for the bees to fill again.

Throughout Medieval times the monasteries were involved in honey production and Britain has a strong tradition of honey production. Indeed the Druids called this country 'the Honey Isle of Beli'. Perhaps bee-keeping was encouraged by it being the only sweetener available at the time. It is also, of course, a vital ingredient of the old English drink, mead, which was widely drunk in the Middle Ages before ale and wine became popular. Beeswax was another vital commodity, particularly in church where it was used to make candles and give a clear, smoke-free, light.

Even today heather honey is considered to be one of the best in the world and despite the fact that Britain imports a great deal of honey, we still manage to export heather honey to connoisseurs around the world.

CHAPTER 2

NUTRITIONAL UPDATE

Constituents of honey – vitamins – minerals – water – enzymes – pollen – pure and wholesome?

Over 180 constituents have been identified in honey. It is an amazingly complex natural food and it varies according to where the bees collected the nectar and the types of soil the plants grow in. Most of these 180 ingredients are in very minute amounts, since honey is about 75 per cent sugars and 20 per cent water. The remainder consists of vitamins, minerals, traces of pollen, wax, ash, etc. By law honey must contain at least 65 per cent sugar and not more than 25 per cent water and can have no other additives.

Sugars
It is tempting to think of all sweet things being the same, but sugars vary. White table sugar is, in fact, sucrose. The sugars in honey are predominantly dextrose and levulose (also known as fructose). This latter sugar is the sweetest simple sugar and is the reason that honey tastes sweeter than table sugar. The ratio of these two sugars varies from honey to honey and governs how set or runny the honey is. Those high in levulose remain unset for longer than those high in dextrose which sets quickly. All honeys will eventually set, or crystallize, usually within about six weeks of removal from the comb. Commercially, some honeys are heated and stirred to encourage a soft set or to keep them unset. Others which would set with a grainy texture are 'seeded' with fine-textured honey to encourage a smooth fine set.

The fact that these sugars in honey are different to ordinary sucrose is very important. The muscles in the body can use levulose directly, without it being processed by the digestive system. It is converted into glycogen, which provides muscles with instant energy. This is why athletes and performers of all kinds eat honey or mix it with water or milk to drink it. High levels of sucrose in the diet require the body to produce high levels of insulin and this can

13

sometimes cause hypoglycemia. If too much insulin is produced, then the blood sugar level drops, causing a lack of energy, irritability and headaches.

Eating more sugar temporarily solves the problem, giving a boost of energy, but then the level drops again and so a circle is set up. The sugars of honey bypass this problem as insulin is not needed to digest the levulose.

Levulose also improves the body's ability to absorb iron and has been found to be very effective at countering the effects of alcohol on the body, especially when combined with vitamin C. So honey and fruit juice will help alleviate the effects of a hangover.

Honey has fewer calories than sugar too; there are 80 calories per ounce of honey compared with 112 per ounce of sugar. Used sparingly it can be useful in a calorie-controlled diet.

Vitamins

Raw honey certainly does contain small quantities of vitamin C and the B group, many of which are needed to aid the digestion of carbohydrates. They are also involved with depression and mental ill health. However the levels are very low, and once heated and packaged the levels are reduced even further. To get the most benefit, choose honey in the comb, or straight from the bee-keeper, if possible.

Minerals

The minerals in honey vary, since they are determined by the levels in the soil where the plants were growing. Depleted soils have depleted mineral levels. Heather honeys are highest in mineral elements, although even in these, the total amounts are low. However, compare them to the complete lack of minerals in white sugar which is refined, and they certainly make some contribution to the diet.

Generally the amount of minerals we need in our diet are small anyway. They are often lumped together as 'trace elements' since we usually need only traces of them. The effect of mineral levels on general health and fitness is an area only recently being researched, so it would seem wise to ensure that a varied wholesome diet is eaten and to maximize the quantity of minerals taken as naturally as possible.

In honey there are traces of potassium, iron, (which is needed to produce haemoglobin in the blood) and copper, which also helps in proper functioning of the blood. Calcium, (honey has been shown to increase calcium retention in the body) and phosphorus are present and so are sodium and silicon. Manganese and magnesium are both needed to ensure the proper production and activity of enzymes in the body and are present in small quantities. Interestingly enough, in a natural diet based largely on unprocessed foods, the minerals needed to assimilate the natural sugars are usually found with those sugars. Processed sugars that have been stripped of minerals make demands on the body in the digestion of the sugars. Honey, as a naturally sweet product, contains small amounts of chromium and other elements which are used in the digestion of sugars.

Water
Nectar is basically sugars dissolved in water. Part of the reason for storing the nectar in the comb is to allow natural evaporation of the water to take place. Honey in the jar is usually about 20 per cent water and if the level is too high, the honey will ferment.

Enzymes
These come from the bees' honeysacs and are the ingredients that begin the process of changing the nectar into honey. Excess heating destroys these enzymes and in fact minimum enzyme activity levels are laid down under EEC Regulations.

Pollen
There are about 4 million pollen grains in each pound of honey. Although debris is filtered out of the honey the pollen grains still remain. Some enthusiasts claim that pollen in honey has special uses for sufferers from hayfever and asthma. (See Honey Remedies.)

The pollen in the honey is useful as a way of proving where the honey comes from. By checking the pollen grains it contains, the type of flowers can be identified and hence the area. In this way, cheap honey being sold as expensive single flower honey can be identified.

Pure and wholesome?
While honey is a natural product and no additives are allowed, pesticides do worry some bee-keepers. These can

be taken in by the bees and passed on in the honey, as well as sometimes killing the bees. So far, despite some monitoring, there appears to be no substantial problem in respect of the honey. Farmers are generally encouraged to spray crops late at night, or early morning, when few bees are flying, and to warn local bee-keepers so that they can shut the hives.

There are thankfully few bee diseases, but some, like American Foul Brood requires killing off the hive. There have been reports of a very rare form of botulism in honeys from some areas of the world as well.

EEC Regulations on honey are quite strict and since it is a natural product with minimal steps in producing it, there are relatively few opportunities for the removal of the goodness or artificial additions.

CHAPTER 3

HONEY REMEDIES

Honey as a cure for ailments – home honey remedies

Honey has long been used as a cure – all for minor and major ailments. It is a mild antiseptic and certainly seems to have soothing qualities. Folk remedies exist using honey for sore throats, to help heal cuts and as an easily digested food, or in drinks for invalids. It seems to be a mild laxative and diuretic.

In the 17th century it was recommended because 'it cleareth all obstructions of the body' and the Greeks and Romans used to eat it, drink it and use it on wounds and burns. Even today some doctors have tried using honey as a wound dressing and report successful results. This may, in part, be due to the fact that honey is hygroscopic, (water attracting) and so when applied to a wound it draws out the moisture, along with any bacteria as well. It was thought to be good for colds, catarrh and may other ailments. The warmed wax from the honeycomb was used on rheumatic joints to ease them and in fact warm wax treatments are still used by physiotherapists today.

Asthma and hayfever sufferers were encouraged to eat pollen or honey in the comb which contains many pollen grains. The theory behind this is that by choosing pollen from the plants to which you are allergic, you gradually desensitize the body. Again this is similar to the methods of desensitizing injections that can be given to severe hayfever sufferers.

In some countries athletes and others swear by pollen and take pollen supplements to enhance their performance, even the national sporting teams of some countries take pollen en masse.

Other honey products, such as royal jelly and bee brood are sold as well, but there is little evidence to support claims that they are effective 'cure-alls'. In subsistence level cultures the small quantities of protein and vitamins in this type of product may well make an improvement to the general health and welfare of the population. The Australian aboriginnes for instance, eat honey ants, which may make a major contribution to an otherwise meagre diet. However in Western cultures our food intake usually outstrips our needs and we are unlikely to benefit from such additions to our diet.

Certainly many country remedies have a basis of fact and it may be well worth trying some of the more palatable and harmless ones for minor ailments.

HONEY HOME REMEDIES

To ease a sore throat or a troublesome cough
Mix two tablespoons each of honey and glycerine with one tablespoon of lemon juice. Keep the mixture warm and use a little as needed.

An old-fashioned cough remedy
Boil one lemon slowly for ten minutes. This will soften it so that more juice will come out. Cut it in half when cool and squeeze out the juice. Add two tablespoons of glycerine and 100g (4oz) of honey and mix well together. Pour into a bottle and use as required, taking a 5ml spoonful at a time. Shake the bottle before using.

A remedy for chilblains
Mix two tablespoons each of honey and glycerine with the white of an egg and enough cornflour to make a paste. Apply after bathing the feet and allow to dry.

A remedy for sunburn
Mix two tablespoons each of honey, glycerine and lemon juice with one of any favourite toilet water. Shake well in a screw-top jar and apply when needed.

A remedy of hangovers
Mix the juice of a freshly squeezed lemon with a large spoonful of honey and add two ice cubes. Repeat every hour.

Honey paste for chapped hands
Mix the white of an egg, one teaspoon of glycerine, 25g (1oz) of honey and enough barley flour to make a smooth

18

paste. Rub on chapped or dry hands. Leave for 10 minutes, then wash off. This can be kept in the refrigerator and used as needed.

Honey remedies for sleeplessness
Stir one or two teaspoonfuls of honey into a glass of milk (warm) and drink just before going to bed. The milk can be cold during the summer if preferred.

Take a teaspoonful of honey with a tablespoonful of cider vinegar in a glass of water last thing at night.

Antiseptic honey gargle
Take a handful of freshly gathered sage leaves and chop roughly. Place in a bowl, then pour over 600ml (1 pint) of boiling water and steep for 10–15 minutes. Strain and stir in one tablespoon of honey. Use warm as a gargle.

Honey to relieve hayfever
Hayfever sufferers are advised to chew local honeycomb or honey cappings at least once a day for a month before the pollen count is due to start, and increase the dose during an attack. This is because the very pollen to which they are allergic is nearby and when they eat honey containing it, they are immunizing themselves. Honey from another area might not contain the proper pollen.

Quick pick-me-up
Add one teaspoonful of honey to a glass of warm water and drink whenever needed. Particularly useful mid-morning or as a light breakfast.

CHAPTER 4

COOKING WITH HONEY

Quick tips for cooking with honey – preserving with honey

***To replace sugar in a recipe with honey use 30ml of honey in place of each 25g sugar and then reduce any other liquid in the recipe by a quarter.

***Darker honeys go well in gingerbread, fruit cake and chocolate cakes. Lighter honeys are best in cakes and biscuits.

***Heat destroys delicate flavours in honey so use the cheaper honeys for cooking.

***Cakes made with honey will have a heavier texture but will be more moist and keep longer than those made with sugar.

***To measure honey, dip the metal spoon in hot water, then scoop up the honey and it will slide off easily into the mixture.

***Liquid honey is easiest to incorporate into a cake mixture.

***When adding honey to butter or margarine, beat the fat well until soft then pour the honey in a fine stream, beating all the time. This gives good volume and texture.

***Substitute honey for sugar when stewing fruits for a delicate flavour and attractive colour.

***Substitute one teaspoonful of honey for sugar in french dressing, for a light sharp salad dressing.

***Honey is good trickled onto muesli in the summer or porridge in the winter.

***Use honey instead of sugar to sweeten custards and sauces.

Preserving with honey

Honey is an excellent preservative for fruit and may be used in place of sugar. Fruit bottled in syrup retains its colour, texture and flavour exceptionally well and the syrup provides a ready-made sauce for serving. A pale, mild honey should be used, as the taste is less strong.

To make the syrup:
1. use $\frac{1}{3}$ honey to $\frac{2}{3}$ water
2. dissolve the honey in warm water
3. fill each jar of prepared fruit with the syrup.

Apricots: Take one hour to bring to 65°C (160°F) and maintain this temperature as near as possible for two hours.

Peaches: (Freestone) Bring slowly to 75°C (180°F) then allow the temperature to fall to 65°C (160°F) and maintain as near as possible for $2\frac{1}{2}$ hours, counting from the time when 75°C (180°F) was reached.

Pears: Bring slowly to 85°C (200°F) then allow the temperature to fall to 75°C (180°F) and maintain as near as possible for $2\frac{1}{2}$ hours, counting from the time when 85°C (200°F) was reached.

Plums, (greengage), apples, rhubarb: Bring slowly to 75°C (180°F) and maintain this temperature as near as possible for $2\frac{1}{2}$ hours.

PEARS VINAIGRETTE

Serves 4

2 ripe dessert pears
Vinaigrette dressing (see
    page 28)

Lettuce
Freshly ground black
    pepper

1   Peel, core and halve the pears lengthways.
2   Arrange each half on a lettuce leaf, pour over the vinaigrette dressing and spinkle with black pepper.

BAKED GAMMON WITH ORANGE HONEY GLAZE

Serves 4

Buy a neat round gammon joint and cut it across in slices at least 2cm (1in) thick. Alternatively, if you know a delicatessen where they slice their own ham, cajole them into cutting you four 2cm (1in) slices.

Glaze:
1 can frozen concentrated orange juice
4 tablespoons clear liquid honey

1   Take a large baking tray and place the gammon slices in it.
2   Dilute the orange concentrate to make 600ml (1 pint) of liquid and pour it over the slices. Bake at 180°C/350°F/ Gas Mark 4 for 1 hour.
3   Remove the tray from the oven and brush the slices with honey. Return the tray to the oven for 10 minutes to set the glaze. Serve immediately.

HONEY DUCK

Serves 6

1 duck, trussed and drawn

Stuffing:
450g (1lb) pork
   sausagemeat
50g (2oz) fresh
   breadcrumbs
Grated peel of 1 orange
$\frac{1}{2}$ teaspoon mixed herbs
Seasoning

Glaze:
1 tablespoon of clear liquid
   honey
Juice of 1 orange

Gravy:
Giblets
300ml ($\frac{1}{2}$ pint) stock
Wholemeal flour
Seasoning

Garnish:
Orange slices
Watercress

1   Mix ingredients for stuffing and pack into duck, sewing or skewering down the loose skin so that it doesn't come out during cooking.

2   Place the duck in a roasting tin and prick the skin all over with a large needle to allow the fat to escape. Rub the skin with sea salt and roast in a fairly hot oven (200°C/400°F/Gas Mark 6) for 30 minutes, then reduce the heat to 180°C/350°F/Gas Mark 4 and cook for another $1\frac{1}{2}$ hours until nearly done.

3   Glaze with honey and orange juice and return to the oven for not more than 15 minutes.

4   Prepare stock by simmering the giblets in 300ml ($\frac{1}{2}$ pint) water. Strain. When the duck is cooked take the drippings from the roasting tin, make a roux with a little flour and stir in the stock. Bring to the boil and simmer until thickened. Adjust seasoning.

5   Garnish with watercress and orange slices.

GRANOLA

Makes 12 servings

450g (1lb) rolled oats
50g (2oz) sunflower seeds
50g (2oz) desiccated
   coconut, unsweetened

100g (4oz) hazelnuts
8 tablespoons clear honey
6 tablespoons safflower oil
1 teaspoon vanilla essence

1 Mix the rolled oats, sunflower seeds, coconut and chopped nuts together. Stir in the honey, safflower oil and vanilla essence.

2 Spread the mixture thinly over two lightly greased baking trays. Bake in a preheated oven at 180°C/350°F/Gas Mark 4, for 20–25 minutes, turning occasionally, so that the oats are evenly browned.

3 Cool, then store in sealed jars or containers for up to one month. Serve with milk or yoghurt.

KIPPER COLESLAW

Serves 2–3

½ small white cabbage
175ml (6fl oz) natural
  yoghurt
3 tablespoons mayonnaise
  (see page 59)
225g (8oz) kipper fillets

Freshly ground black
  pepper
Tomato slices for garnish

Marinade:
100ml (4fl oz) white wine
2 teaspoons olive oil

1   Marinate the kipper fillets overnight.

2   Shred cabbage finely and coat with Honey and Lemon
    Dressing (see page 43), sprinkling with black pepper.

3   Drain and skin kipper fillets, roll up into strips and
    arrange on top of the cabbage.

4   Garnish with tomato slices and serve with lettuce.

LEMON CRAB
Serves 4

1 small tin crabmeat
1 punnet cress
3 hard-boiled eggs
Freshly ground black
   pepper

1 teaspoon lemon juice
Grated peel of 1 lemon
150ml ($\frac{1}{4}$ pint) mayonnaise
   (see page 59)

1   Cut, wash and drain the cress, sprinkling a little at the bottom of 4 sundae glasses.

2   Drain the crabmeat and chop it coarsely. Shell and chop the eggs and mix lightly with the crabmeat. Season with black pepper.

3   Add lemon juice and grated peel to mayonnaise, then add to eggs and crabmeat, mixing well.

4   Pile mixture into glasses and sprinkle remaining cress round the edge.

HONEY GLAZED BACON

Serves 6

Boned forehock of bacon
   $1\frac{1}{2}$–2kg   (3–4lb)
bay leaf

Blade mace
2 peppercorns
2–3 cloves

Glaze:
3 tablespoons clear liquid
   honey
Juice of 1 orange (or 2–3
   tablespoons pineapple
   juice)

Gravy:
300ml ($\frac{1}{2}$ pint) bacon stock
1 level tablespoon cornflour

1   Roll and tie bacon joint and cover with water in a large
casserole, adding bay, mace, peppercorns and cloves.
Bring to the boil and simmer for 50 minutes. Drain,
reserving 300ml ($\frac{1}{2}$ pint) strained stock for gravy.

2 Prepare the glaze by mixing honey and orange juice. Score the bacon rind by cutting in a diamond pattern, place it in a roasting tin and pour the glaze over slowly so that it soaks into the incisions in the rind.

3 Roast at 180°C/350°F/Gas Mark 4 for up to 1 hour (until tender), basting occasionally.

4 Remove string before serving and pour pan drippings over the joint.

5 Make gravy from stock and cornflour, seasoning well. You can also make your gravy from the pan drippings, but it will be rather sweet.

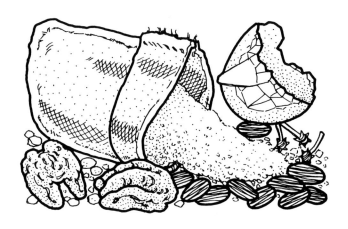

VINAIGRETTE

6 tablespoons olive oil
2 tablespoons tarragon vinegar
2 teaspoons honey
$\frac{1}{2}$ teaspoon chopped capers
$\frac{1}{2}$ teaspoon chopped onion
Good pinch basil, fennel and dill
$\frac{1}{2}$ teaspoon chopped mint

1 Combine all ingredients and stir well. Stir again before serving.

CHICKEN CELESTE
Serves 4

4 chicken pieces
Sea salt and freshly ground
  black pepper
Few rashers fat bacon
3 tablespoons clear liquid
  honey

2 level tablespoons French
  mustard
1 teaspoon curry powder
  (or to taste)
1 crushed clove garlic

1 Skin the chicken pieces, lay them in a fire-proof dish,
   sprinkle with salt and pepper and cover with bacon.

2 Mix other ingredients and pour over. Bake at 180°C/
   350°F/Gas Mark 4 for about 1 hour until pieces are
   tender, turning them over at half time and basting
   occasionally.

3 Serve with plain gravy and a sauce made from the pan
   drippings, though this may be a little sweet for some
   tastes.

SALAD NIÇOISE
Serves 4

6 small potatoes
100g (4oz) whole green
    beans
1 lettuce
Vinaigrette (see page 28)
1 can tuna fish or salmon
1 can anchovy fillets

2 hard-boiled eggs,
    quartered
1 onion, sliced
4 tomatoes, quartered
12 black olives, pitted
1 green pepper, thinly
    sliced

1 Boil the potatoes in their jackets until just tender; peel
   and slice. Cook beans, leaving them whole, and drain.
   Put the potatoes and beans in the refrigerator to chill.

2 Wash the lettuce and shake well to dry. Separate the
   leaves and line a large bowl with them. Sprinkle with
   vinaigrette dressing, also sprinkling the potatoes and
   beans.

3 Drain the fish and separate into chunks.

4 Layer all ingredients on top of the lettuce. The enjoyment of this salad can be considerably heightened by the artistic arrangements of the ingredients, and you have a good assortment of colours and textures to make it attractive. Save the olives, egg quarters and tomato quarters for the top. Sprinkle again with vinaigrette and chill before serving.

TUNA SALAD
Serves 4

1 can tuna fish
1 can butter beans, drained
4 spring onions, finely chopped

3 tablespoons vinaigrette (see page 28)
Sea salt and freshly ground black pepper

1 Divide the tuna fish into chunks with a fork. Add to beans and onions or chives and mix well. Moisten with vinaigrette dressing and season. Serve with lettuce.

SALAD CAPRI
Serves 4

150g (6oz) long-grain brown rice
1 green pepper
4 large tomatoes
600ml (1 pint) prawns

1 small can whole-kernel sweetcorn
Vinaigrette (see page 28)
Sea salt and freshly ground black pepper

1 Boil the rice, drain, rinse and cool.

2 Remove seeds and core from the pepper, cover with water, bring to the boil, simmer for 5 minutes, drain, cool and cut into strips.

3 Cover the tomatoes with boiling water, leave for 1 minute, drain, skin and cut into slices. Shell prawns, drain sweet corn.

4 Saving a few prawns for garnish, mix all ingredients with vinaigrette. Season. Serve with remaining prawns.

SWEET & SOUR CABBAGE
Serves 4–6

1 small or ½ large red
  cabbage
1–2 tablespoons vegetable
  oil
1 large onion
2 cooking apples
2 tablespoons clear honey
2 tablespoons red wine or
  cider vinegar

¼ teaspoon cinnamon
  (optional)
¼ teaspoon ground cloves
  (optional)
¼ teaspoon allspice
  (optional)
Freshly ground black
  pepper

1 Discard any damaged leaves from the cabbage. Cut
   away the white core and then shred the cabbage finely
   across the leaves. Rinse in cold salted water and drain.

2 Heat the oil in a large heavy-based saucepan (red cabbage is bulky to begin with but cooks down) add the

peeled and chopped onion and fry until it begins to look transparent.

3 Peel, core and chop the apples and add to the pan with the cabbage, honey, wine vinegar, spice (if using), and a good grinding of black pepper. Turn all the ingredients in the pan to mix, then add sufficient boiling water from a kettle to just cover the base of the pan – about 150ml ($\frac{1}{4}$ pint).

4 Cover the pan with a lid and simmer over low heat for about 1 hour. Stir or shake the pan occasionally. When cooked and ready to serve all the liquid will have evaporated. Serve hot.

FRESH FRUIT SALAD

Serves 6–8

4 tablespoons clear honey	1 small pineapple
150ml ($\frac{1}{4}$ pint) water	1 kiwifruit
2 oranges	2 red skinned eating apples
1 small bunch white grapes	2 firm eating pears
1 small bunch black grapes	1 banana
225g (8oz) plums or strawberries	Juice of 2 lemons

1   Place the water and honey in a small pan and heat gently until the honey has dissolved. Set aside to cool.

2   Peel the oranges, removing all the pith, and divide into segments. Wash and halve the grapes, removing the pips.

3   Wash the plums, if using, halve and remove their stones. Wash and hull the strawberries, if used.

4   Peel the pineapple with a sharp knife and cut the flesh into sections, discarding the central core. Peel and cut kiwifruit into fine slices.

5   Cut the apples into quarters and remove core. Slice thinly and place in lemon juice to prevent browning. Peel pears, remove core and cut into small chunks, mix with the apples and lemon juice, peel and slice the banana and mix with the juice also.

6   Mix all the fruit together in a bowl and pour over the syrup. Chill until required.

HONEYED SHORTBREAD

Makes 8 pieces

100g (4oz) butter
50g (2oz) set honey
150g (6oz) wholemeal flour

25g (1oz) brown rice flour
Grated rind of 1 lemon

1   Cream the butter and honey together until soft. Stir in the flours, the grated lemon rind and work the mixture to give a soft dough.

2   Press the dough into a well-floured shortbread mould or an 18cm (7in) sandwich tin. Turn out on to a baking tray.

3   Mark the top of the dough with a sharp knife, dividing it into 8 wedges. Prick the dough all over with a fork and crimp the edges. Chill for about 1 hour.

4   Bake the shortbread in a preheated oven at 150°C/300°F/Gas Mark 2, for about 40 minutes, or until just beginning to brown. Cut into pieces while warm, but leave to cool in the tin.

Note: The rice flour is a traditional ingredient of shortbread, but it can be omitted, in which case use 175g (6oz) wholemeal flour.

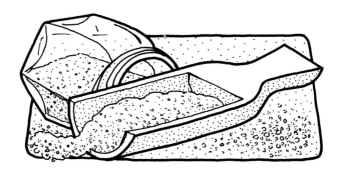

BAKED HONEY CUSTARD

Serves 4–6

3 eggs, lightly beaten
4 tablespoons clear honey
Pinch of sea salt

750ml (1¼ pints) milk
½ teaspoon vanilla essence
A little grated nutmeg

1 To the beaten eggs add the honey, milk, salt and vanilla essence. Mix thoroughly.

2 Strain and pour the mixture into a greased ovenproof dish, or six individual custard cups. Grate a little nutmeg on to the surface of each.

3 Cover the bottom of a shallow baking tin with 1cm (½ inch) of water; place the dishes in the tin and bake in a preheated moderate oven at 180°C/350°F/Gas Mark 4 until the custard is just set – about 45 minutes for a large dish and 30 minutes for the small cups.

4 Serve warm, or chill in the refrigerator before serving.

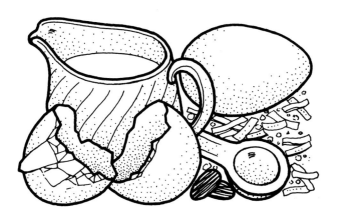

WHISKY SYLLABUB

Serves 4–6

| 4–5 tablespoons whisky | 4 tablespoons clear honey |
| 1 tablespoon lemon juice | 300ml ($\frac{1}{2}$ pint) double cream |

1 Mix together the whisky, lemon juice and honey in a bowl.

2 Pour in the cream, then whisk, preferably with an electric mixer, until the mixture stands in soft peaks. Pile into individual glasses and chill well. Serve with Honey Ratafia Biscuits (see page 57).

FRENCH APPLE FLAN
Serves 8

Pastry:
175g (6oz) wholemeal flour
Pinch of sea salt
75g (3oz) butter
1 teaspoon clear honey
1 egg yolk
Cold water to mix

Filling:
900g (2lb) cooking apples

2 tablespoons water
5 tablespoons clear honey
Grated rind and juice of 1
  lemon
25g (1oz) butter
$\frac{1}{2}$ teaspoon ground
  cinnamon
2 eating apples

1   Place the flour and salt into a bowl and rub in the butter
    until the mixture resembles breadcrumbs in consistency.
    Stir in the honey. Beat the egg yolk with a little water
    and mix into the flour, adding more water if necessary
    to make a soft dough. Wrap it in greaseproof paper and
    refrigerate for 30 minutes.

2   Meanwhile, prepare the filling. Peel and core the cooking apples. Slice and simmer gently with the water in a covered pan until soft. Add 3 tablespoons honey, the grated lemon rind, butter and cinnamon and cook uncovered until reduced to a thick purée. Allow the apple purée to cool

3   Roll the pastry out on a lightly floured surface and line a 20cm (8in) fluted flan ring placed on a baking sheet. Bake blind in a preheated oven at 200°C/400°F/Gas Mark 6, for 10–15 minutes.

4   Pour the apple purée into the flan case. Core the eating apples but do not peel them. Cut into thin even slices and toss in the lemon juice.

5   Arrange the apple slices neatly in overlapping circles on top of the purée. Bake in a preheated oven at 190°C/375°F/Gas Mark 5, for 30 minutes, or until the apples are cooked and lightly browned.

6   Place 2 tablespoons honey in a pan with the lemon juice remaining from the apples and heat gently until the honey dissolves. Brush or spoon over the cooked flan to glaze.

PEAR AND HONEY SORBET

Serves 4

900g (2lb) pears
Grated rind and juice of 1
   lemon

3 tablespoons clear honey
1 egg white

1   Peel, quarter and core the pears.

2   Slice the pears into a saucepan. Add the lemon rind and juice and the honey. Cover the pan and cook over low heat, stirring occasionally, for 10–15 minutes, or until the pears are tender. Sieve or liquidise to a smooth purée.

3   Pour the purée into a shallow container (such as an empty ice-cream tub) and place in the freezer for about 1 hour, or until half frozen.

4   When the purée is half frozen, remove it from the freezer
    and whisk with an electric beater. Whisk the egg white
    until stiff and fold into the purée. Return the sorbet to
    the freezer and freeze until firm.

5   Transfer to the refrigerator 20–30 minutes before serv-
    ing, to soften, then scoop into 4 individual glasses.

HONEY BUTTERSCOTCH

Makes $\frac{3}{4}$kg (1$\frac{1}{2}$lb)

450g (1lb) clear honey
225g (8oz) butter

$\frac{1}{2}$ teaspoon sea salt
Vanilla essence

1 Put the honey in a saucepan and bring to the boil, stirring all the time, until thick and a small amount dropped in cold water will harden instantly. Remove from the heat and stir in the melted butter, salt and vanilla essence.

2 Pour the mixture into a well-greased shallow tin and mark into small squares when almost set. When cold break it up into squares and wrap in waxed or cellophane paper because the butterscotch becomes very sticky if exposed to the air.

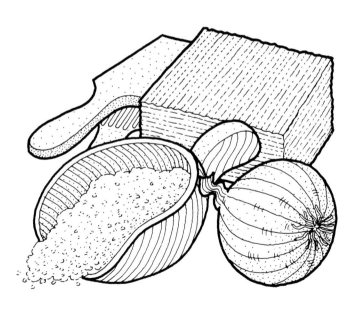

APRICOT AND WALNUT LOAF

Makes 1 loaf

225g (8oz) wholemeal flour
225g (8oz) unbleached
  white flour
1 teaspoon sea salt
25g (1oz) butter or
  margarine

15g ($\frac{1}{2}$oz) fresh yeast
300ml ($\frac{1}{2}$ pint) warm water
2 tablespoons set honey
75g (3oz) walnuts, chopped
175g (6oz) dried apricots,
  chopped

1   Mix the flours and salt in a bowl; rub in the fat.

2   Cream the yeast with a little of the water and leave until frothy. Add to the flour with the remaining water, the honey, nuts and fruit. Mix well to form a dough.

3   Turn on to a lightly floured surface and knead for 5–10 minutes until smooth and elastic. Place the dough in a greased bowl and cover with oiled polythene. Leave to rise in a warm place for about 1$\frac{1}{2}$ hours, until doubled in size.

4   Turn risen dough on to a lightly floured surface and knead again for 2–3 minutes. Shape and place in a greased 1kg (2lb) loaf tin.

5   Cover with oiled polythene and leave to prove until dough is just rounded over the top of the tin (about 30 minutes). Bake in a preheated oven at 220°C/425°F/Gas Mark 7, for 25–30 minutes, or until it is golden and sounds hollow when tapped underneath. Cool on a wire rack.

Note: For a sticky topped loaf brush with warmed apricot jam when baked.

HONEY AND LEMON DRESSING

Makes 150ml ($\frac{1}{4}$ pint)

4 tablespoons lemon juice
2 tablespoons clear honey
3 tablespoons olive oil

Sea salt and freshly ground
  black pepper

1   Put all the ingredients in a screw-topped jar, adding salt and pepper to taste. Shake well to blend before serving.

BAKED SPICED GRAPEFRUIT
Serves 4

These spiced hot grapefruit halves make a refreshing start or finish to a meal.

2 large grapefruit
2 dessertspoons clear
  honey

2 tablespoons sherry
$\frac{1}{2}$ teaspoon mixed spice or
  cinnamon

1   Cut the grapefruits in half horizontally. Using a grapefruit knife, cut around the segments to loosen them. Remove and discard the pips.

2   Put the grapefruit halves into an ovenproof dish. Drizzle the honey and sherry over the portions and sprinkle with a little cinnamon on top.

3   Bake in a preheated moderately hot oven 190°C/375°F/ Gas Mark 5, for 10–15 minutes, or until heated through. Serve hot.

BUTTERSCOTCH SUNDAE
Serves 4

Brick vanilla ice cream
3 bananas, sliced

100g (4oz) chopped walnuts
Honey Butterscotch (page 42)

1 Place alternate layers of ice cream, sliced bananas and chopped walnuts into sundae cups or glasses, finishing with ice cream. Chill.

2 Just before serving, top with butterscotch broken very fine with a toffee hammer, or crushed between two layers of greaseproof paper with a rolling pin.

CAROB YULE LOG
Serves 6–8

For Roll:
3 large eggs
100g (4 oz) clear honey
75g (3oz) wholemeal flour
25g (1oz) carob or cocoa
  powder
2 dessertspoons hot water
For Filling:
175g (6oz) low-fat soft white
  cheese

2 drops vanilla essence
1 teaspoon decaffeinated
  coffee powder, dissolved
  in a little water
1–2 tablespoons clear
  honey
15g ($\frac{1}{2}$oz) carob or cocoa
  powder
A little yoghurt if necessary

1   Whisk the eggs and honey together until thick and hold-
    ing trail of whisk for 3 seconds.

2   Sieve together the wholemeal flour and carob powder
    and fold into the whisked mixture using a metal spoon.
    Add the hot water and fold in lightly.

3   Pour into a lined and greased 23 x 33cm (9 x 13in) Swiss roll tin. Bake in a preheated oven at 220°C/425°F/Gas Mark 7 for 12–15 minutes until cooked and springy to the touch.

4   Turn out immediately on to a piece of greaseproof paper. (To help make the sponge pliable place the greaseproof paper over a damp tea towel.)

5   Trim off the crusty edges and make a light cut into the sponge across one short end. Place another piece of greaseproof paper over sponge and roll up from cut end, leave until quite cold.

6   Beat together the filling ingredients. Unroll the cake and spread half the cheese filling over, almost to the edges. Roll up carefully.

7   Spread the remaining half of the filling on top of the log and make a bark pattern using the back of a fork.

FARMHOUSE FRUIT CAKE

Serves 8–10

175g (6oz) butter or margarine
175g (6oz) clear honey
Grated rind of 1 lemon
3 eggs, lightly beaten
225g (8oz) wholemeal flour
2 teaspoons baking powder
1 teaspoon mixed spice
100g (4oz) raisins
100g (4oz) sultanas
100g (4oz) currants
50g (2oz) dried apricots, chopped
50g (2oz) cut mixed peel
25g (1oz) ground almonds
25g (1oz) split blanched almonds

1   Cream together the butter, honey and lemon rind until light and soft. Gradually beat in the eggs, adding a little flour to prevent the mixture curdling.

2   Sift the remaining flour with the baking powder and spice over the mixture and fold in gently, adding the bran from the sieve at the end.

3   Stir in the dried fruits, mixed peel and ground almonds. Turn into a greased and lined 20cm (8in) round cake tin and smooth the top with a palette knife leaving a slight hollow in the middle so that the cake will rise evenly. Arrange the split blanched almonds neatly around the edge.

4   Bake in a preheated moderate oven, 160°C/325°F/Gas Mark 3, for about 2–2½ hours. Cover the top of the cake with a piece of greaseproof paper after 1 hour to prevent the top from burning. When the cake is cooked, a metal skewer inserted into the middle should come out clean.

5   Let the cake stand in the tin for about 10 minutes before removing it from the tin and taking off the greaseproof paper. Cool on a wire rack. This cake stores well in an airtight tin.

FRUIT AND NUT FLAPJACKS
Makes 16 bars

These crunchy, sticky bars will keep well for up to 2 weeks if they are stored in an airtight container.

75g (3oz) butter or margarine	100g (4oz) set honey
50g (2oz) raisins	50g (2oz) walnuts, chopped
	175g (6oz) rolled oats

1 Melt the honey with the butter or margarine in a saucepan over low heat.

2 Stir in the raisins, walnuts and oats and mix thoroughly.

3 Turn into a greased 18 x 28cm (7 x 11in) shallow tin and smooth the top with a palette knife.

4 Bake in a preheated moderate oven, 180°C/350°F/Gas Mark 4, for 25–30 minutes. Cut into bars while still warm. Cool in the tin until the bars are hard, then put on a wire rack.

STUFFED BAKED APPLES

Serves 4

4 large cooking apples, cored
2 tablespoons clear honey
40g (1½oz) raisins
40g (1½oz) dried apricots, chopped

25g (1oz) chopped mixed nuts
1 teaspoon ground cinnamon
4 tablespoons cider or water

1   Make a shallow cut round the middle of each apple to prevent the skins from bursting during cooking.

2   Mix the honey with the dried fruit, nuts and cinnamon. Use to fill the apple cavities, pressing down firmly.

3   Place the apples in a shallow ovenproof dish with the cider or water in the base.

4   Bake in a preheated moderate oven at 180°C/350°F/Gas Mark 4, for about 45 minutes, or until the apples are tender. Serve hot or cold with pouring cream, custard or yoghurt.

BANANA AND HONEY SHAKE

Serves 2–3

3 ripe bananas
2 tablespoons clear honey
300 ml (½ pint) milk

1   Slice the bananas into a liquidiser or food processor. Add the honey with the milk and blend until smooth.

2   Pour into individual tall glasses. Place a couple of drinking straws in each glass and serve with a banana slice or two on the top.

HONEY-FRIED BANANAS

Serves 4

40g (½oz) butter
2 tablespoons clear honey

Juice of 1 lemon
4 bananas

1   Melt the butter in a frying pan. Add the honey and lemon juice.

2   Peel the bananas and cut in half lengthwise, add to the pan and cook, turning once, until browned on both sides. Serve with the remaining liquid poured over the top.

HONEY BUTTER

100g (4oz) unsalted butter
100g (4oz) clear honey
1 teaspoon lemon juice

1   Cream the butter till soft, and gradually beat in the honey. Add the lemon juice slowly and blend until smooth.

2   Store in the refrigerator and use as a spread for wholemeal toast, pancakes or waffles.

HONEY FRENCH DRESSING

Makes 250ml (8fl oz)

175ml (6fl oz) olive oil
4 tablespoons wine vinegar
1 clove of garlic, peeled and crushed

1 teaspoon French mustard
1 teaspoon clear honey
Sea salt and freshly ground black pepper

1   Put all the ingredients in a screw-topped jar, adding salt and pepper to taste. Shake well to blend before serving.

CHOCOLATE HONEY COOKIES
Makes 20

2 teaspoons clear honey
225g (8oz) butter or
  margarine

6 tablespoons carob
  powder
225g (8oz) semi-sweet
  biscuits, crushed

1 Place honey, butter or margarine and carob powder in
   a saucepan and heat until the ingredients melt, stirring
   all the time. Add crushed biscuits, mixing well in, until
   smooth.

2 Pour the mixture into a greased shallow tin and leave to
   set. When cool cut into bars or shapes. The biscuits can
   then be decorated with icing if desired.

Note: This is such an easy recipe that it is very suitable
for children to try, especially as there is very little heat
required and no danger of anything boiling over.

PEANUT-BUTTER COOKIES

Makes about 30

120ml (4fl oz) vegetable oil
175g (6oz) clear honey
175g (6oz) crunchy peanut
  butter
1 egg, beaten

100g (4oz) porridge oats
225g (8oz) wholemeal flour
50g (2oz) desiccated
  coconut unsweetened

1 In a large bowl mix together the oil, honey, peanut butter, and egg until well blended.

2 Add the dry ingredients and mix thoroughly.

3 Drop heaped teaspoons on to a baking tray and flatten to about 6mm ($\frac{1}{4}$in) with a fork. Bake in a preheated oven at 180°C/350°F/Gas Mark 4, for about 10–12 minutes. Cool on a wire rack.

SUMMER PUDDING

Serves 4–6

675g (1½lb) mixed summer fruit – raspberries, hulled strawberries, stoned red or black cherries, red or black currants – washed

8–10 slices bread, without crust
100g (4oz) clear honey
Whipped cream or custard to serve

1   Line the base and sides of a 900ml (1½ pint) soufflé dish or pudding basin with the slices of bread, shaping them so that they fit close together.

2   Put the washed fruit into a heavy-based pan and drizzle over the honey. Bring to the boil over low heat, then cook (for 5–10 minutes) until the fruit is soft and the juice starts to run.

3   Reserving 3 tablespoons of the juice, spoon the contents of the pan into the bread-lined basin and cover the top with the rest of the bread.

4   Place a saucer or plate with a 450g (1lb) weight on it on top of the pudding. Leave in a cool place or in the refrigerator overnight.

5   Just prior to serving, turn the pudding out on to a serving plate. Pour the reserved juice over any parts of the bread that have not been soaked through and coloured by the fruit juices. Serve with a light Custard sauce (page 37) or lightly whipped cream.

HONEY COOKIES

Makes 20

75g (3oz) butter or
  margarine
100g (4oz) set honey
225g (8oz) wholemeal flour
1 level teaspoon baking
  powder

Pinch of sea salt
50g (2oz) muscovado sugar
1 level teaspoon cinnamon
1 egg, beaten

1 Put the butter and honey in a pan and heat gently until the butter has melted.

2 Sift the flour, baking powder, salt and cinnamon into a bowl, add the warm honey mixture and the beaten egg. Mix well.

3 Place heaped teaspoonfuls of the mixture well apart on a greased baking sheet. Bake in a preheated moderate oven at 180°C/350°F/Gas Mark 4 for about 15 minutes. Leave to cool for 2 minutes then transfer to a wire rack to cool completely.

4 Store in an airtight tin for up to one week.

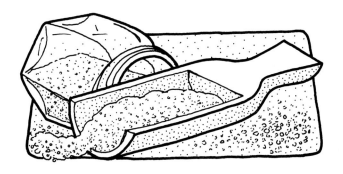

GINGERBREAD

100g (4oz) butter or margarine
50g (2oz) honey
175g (6oz) molasses or black treacle
225g (8oz) wholemeal flour
1 teaspoon ground cinnamon
2 teaspoons ground ginger

2 level teaspoons baking powder
50g (2oz) chopped mixed nuts
$\frac{1}{2}$ teaspoon bicarbonate of soda
200ml ($\frac{1}{3}$ pint) warm milk
2 eggs, beaten

1   Place the butter, honey and molasses in a pan and heat gently until melted.

2   Mix the flour, spices, nuts and baking powder in a large mixing bowl, make a well in the centre and add the warmed molasses mixture and the beaten eggs.

3   Blend the bicarbonate of soda and milk together and stir into the mixture.

4   Pour the runny mixture into a lined and greased 23cm (9 inch) square cake tin and bake in a preheated moderate oven, 180°C/350°F/Gas Mark 4, for 45–60 minutes, until well risen and firm to the touch. Cool slightly before turning out on to a wire rack:

HONEY RATAFIAS
Makes 25

2 egg whites	A few drops of almond
100g (4oz) ground almonds	essence
100g (4oz) clear honey	Rice paper sheets

1   Beat the egg whites until stiff. Carefully fold in the almonds, a few drops of almond essence, and the honey.

2   Line 2 baking sheets with rice paper. Put teaspoonfuls of the mixture on the paper, leaving plenty of space between them since they will spread during cooking.

3 Bake in a preheated oven, 180°C/350°F/Gas Mark 4, for about 15 minutes, until golden brown. Cool slightly, remove from the tins, and tear or cut around each one to remove the excess rice paper.

HONEY WHOLEWHEAT BREAD

Makes 1 loaf

750g (1¾lb) wholemeal flour
½ teaspoon sea salt
15g (½oz) fresh yeast
450ml (¾ pint) warm water

3 tablespoons set honey
50g (2oz) butter or
   margarine, melted
1 tablespoon sesame seeds

1 Mix the flour and salt together in a bowl. Cream the yeast with little of the water and leave until frothy. Add the flour with the remaining water, honey and melted butter; mix to a dough.

2 Turn on to a floured surface and knead for 8–10 minutes until smooth and elastic. Place in a greased bowl and cover with oiled polythene. Leave to rise in a warm place for about 2 hours, until doubled in size.

3 Turn on to a floured surface and knead for a few minutes. Form into a fairly wide roll and place on a greased baking sheet. Brush with water and sprinkle with the sesame seeds. Cover with oiled polythene and leave to prove for about 30 minutes, until almost doubled in size. Remove polythene.

4 Bake in a preheated oven 220°C/425°F/Gas Mark 7, for 15 minutes. Lower the temperature to 190°C/375°F/Gas Mark 5, and bake for a further 20–25 minutes, until the bread sounds hollow when tapped. Cool on a wire rack.

HONEY MAYONNAISE

2 eggs
2 tablespoons clear liquid
   honey
1 teaspoon made mustard
Sea salt and freshly ground
   black pepper

300ml ($\frac{1}{2}$ pint) olive oil
1 teaspoon tarragon
   vinegar
Juice of 2 lemons

1 Break the eggs into a basin, making sure that only the yolks slide in and the whites remain behind in the shell.

2 Add honey, mustard, salt and pepper. Stir with a wooden spoon to mix.

3 Beat in the oil drop by drop, always beating the same way (don't change hands even if your arm feels as if it were going to drop off), until the mixture takes on the consistency of batter. If it curdles, and won't improve with beating, beat another egg yolk in another basin and add it to the mayonnaise gradually, beating all the time.

4 When the mayonnaise is quite stiff add the vinegar and lemon juice, stirring it in.

HONEY BUNS

Makes 12

100g (4oz) margarine
100g (4oz) clear honey
2 eggs, beaten
175g (6 oz) 81% self-raising
  wheatmeal flour

Finely grated rind of 1
  lemon
A little milk

1 Cream the margarine and honey together until light and fluffy, then gradually beat in the eggs a spoonful at a time.

2 Fold in the flour, the lemon rind and enough milk to give a soft, dropping consistency.

3 Divide the mixture equally between twelve paper bun cases, or into lightly oiled hollows of a bun sheet. Bake in a preheated moderately hot oven, 190°C/375°F/Gas Mark 5, for 15–20 minutes. Cool the buns on a wire rack.

CAROTTES RAPEÉS (GRATED CARROT SALAD)

Serves 4–6

750g (1½lb) carrots
1–2 tablespoons snipped
  chives

2 tablespoons chopped
  parsley
6 tablespoons Honey French
Dressing (see page 51)

1 Grate the carrots finely and place them in a bowl with the chives and parsley.

2 Pour over the dressing and toss well.

3 Transfer the salad to a serving dish and chill lightly before serving if preferred.

HONEY GLAZED CARROTS

Serves 4–6 as a side dish

675g (1½lb) young carrots, scrubbed
Rind of ½ lemon
25g (1oz) butter or margarine
300ml (½ pint) vegetable stock or water

1 dessertspoon clear honey
Sea salt and freshly ground black pepper
1 tablespoon chopped parsley

1 Leave the small carrots whole, cut larger ones into halves lengthways.

2 Place in a saucepan with the lemon rind and butter. Add sufficient water or stock to barely cover the carrots.

3 Add the honey and boil briskly, uncovered, until the stock is absorbed and the carrots are glazed – about 10–12 minutes. Season to taste. Serve hot, garnished with chopped parsley.

HONEY LEMONADE

This makes a refreshing drink for hot summer days. Store it in the refrigerator and serve with plenty of ice and a few slices of lemon floating on top.

3 lemons
900ml (1½ pints) boiling water
4 tablespoons clear honey

1 Thinly peel the lemons, and place the rind in a large bowl. Pour on boiling water, cover and leave to stand for 30 minutes.

2 Add the lemon juice, then the honey and stir well to dissolve.

3 Strain and chill before serving.

HONEY LEMON CURD

Makes 675g (1½lbs)

6 eggs
Juice of 3 lemons
Grated rind of 2 lemons

175g (6oz) clear honey
100g (4oz) unsalted butter,
 softened

1 Beat the eggs and lemon juice together and strain into a
   heatproof bowl. Stir in the grated lemon rind, honey and
   butter.

2 Place the bowl over a pan of simmering water. Stir over
   low heat until the mixture thickens and will coat the back
   of a wooden spoon – about 20 minutes.

3 Pour the curd into warmed jars and cover with waxed
   discs while hot. When cold, seal with cellophane discs
   or lids. Store in a cool dry place and use within 2–3
   weeks.

Note: This recipe is best when a lightly flavoured honey is
   used.

HONEY FRUIT PUNCH
Makes 1.2 litres (2 pints)

4 tablespoons clear honey
300ml ($\frac{1}{2}$ pint) orange juice
150ml ($\frac{1}{4}$ pint) grapefruit
  juice

150ml ($\frac{1}{4}$ pint) lemon juice
600ml (1 pint) water
Slices of orange to garnish

1   Mix the honey with the fruit juices and water in a punch
bowl or jug. Store in the refrigerator until ready to use.

2   Serve in tall glasses with $\frac{1}{2}$ orange slice to garnish.

INDEX